BRUCE McMILLAN

TIME TO...

In memory of F.H.M. Jr.

LOTHROP, LEE & SHEPARD BOOKS · NEW YORK

Copyright © 1989 by Bruce McMillan. All rights reserved. No part of this book may be reproduced or utilized in any form or by any means, electronic or mechanical, including photocopying, recording or by any information storage and retrieval system, without permission in writing from the Publisher. Inquiries should be addressed to Lothrop, Lee & Shepard Books, a division of William Morrow & Company, Inc., 105 Madison Avenue, New York, New York 10016. Printed in the United States of America. First Edition 1 2 3 4 5 6 7 8 9 10

Library of Congress Cataloging in Publication Data McMillan, Bruce. Time to—/by Bruce McMillan.   p.   cm.   Summary: An hour-by-hour introduction to telling time follows the activities of a little boy's day from getting up in the morning to going to bed at night. ISBN 0-688-08855-4.—ISBN 0-688-08856-2 (lib. bdg.) 1. Time—Juvenile literature. 2. Clocks and watches—Juvenile literature.   [1. Time. 2. Clocks and watches.] I. Title.   QB209.5.M38 1989 529—dc19 89-2325 CIP AC

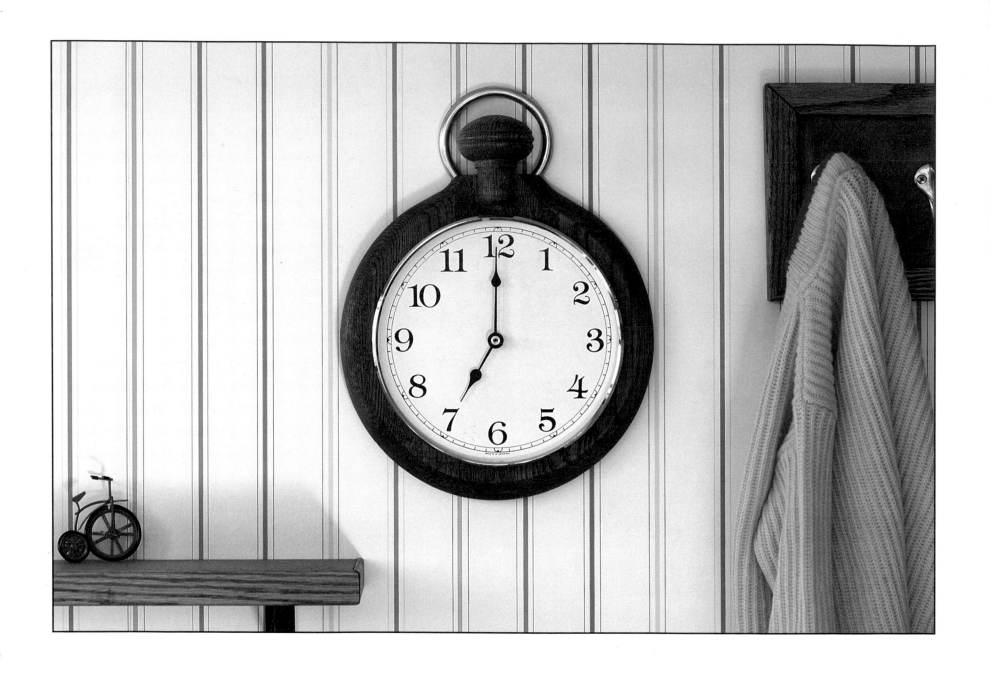

7:00 AM   **SEVEN O'CLOCK IN THE MORNING**

TIME TO . . .

WAKE UP

8:00AM

EIGHT O'CLOCK IN THE MORNING

TIME TO . . .   **EAT BREAKFAST**

9:00AM

NINE O'CLOCK IN THE MORNING

TIME TO . . .   **GO TO SCHOOL**

10:00AM

TEN O'CLOCK IN THE MORNING

TIME TO . . .   **PAINT A PICTURE**

11:00AM

ELEVEN O'CLOCK IN THE MORNING

TIME TO . . .   **PLAY AT RECESS**

12:00PM

TWELVE O'CLOCK NOON

TIME TO . . .   **EAT LUNCH**

1:00 PM   **ONE O'CLOCK IN THE AFTERNOON**

TIME TO . . .   **RIDE IN THE CAR**

2:00 PM

TWO O'CLOCK IN THE AFTERNOON

TIME TO . . .   **GET BOOKS AT THE LIBRARY**

3:00 PM   **THREE O'CLOCK IN THE AFTERNOON**

TIME TO . . .

BUY APPLES AT THE STORE

4:00PM

FOUR O'CLOCK IN THE AFTERNOON

TIME TO . . .   **RIDE A BIKE**

5:00 PM

FIVE O'CLOCK IN THE AFTERNOON

TIME TO . . .   **EAT DINNER**

6:00PM

SIX O'CLOCK IN THE EVENING

TIME TO . . .   **SWING**

7:00 PM

SEVEN O'CLOCK IN THE EVENING

TIME TO . . . **BRUSH**

8:00PM

EIGHT O'CLOCK IN THE EVENING

TIME TO . . .   **READ A BOOK**

9:00PM

NINE O'CLOCK AT NIGHT

TIME TO . . .   **FALL ASLEEP**

Time To… introduces the reader to two aspects of time. First, through clearly sequenced activities, it demonstrates the passage of time. Second, it shows that time can be measured, and how this is done. The hour-by-hour changes on the face of the clock accompanying the picture of each activity allow the reader to observe and participate in the measuring—that is, telling time.

The initial step in learning how to tell time is understanding how to measure time by the hour, the "o'clock." *Time To…* is designed to help the reader master this step. The next step is learning to measure time by the minute with the clock's big hand. Each hour is divided into sixty minutes. The half hour and quarter hour, as shown here, are usually learned first; then five-minute intervals.

Most clocks measure a twenty-four-hour day as two twelve-hour periods, A.M. and P.M. The clock face, digital display, and accompanying text introduce and depict the concept of A.M./P.M.

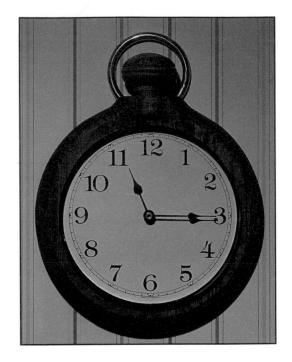

Brian McConnell was photographed with his family: brother Kevin, sister Stephanie, and parents Matt and Dianne. Also photographed were his school friends Daniel Jackson, Kristine Wilson, and Jonathan Bagley. The photographs were taken at Brian's home in Kennebunk, Maine; in Cindy Hayes's class at Cousens School; in the Springvale, Maine, Public Library; in Gile Orchard's store; along Parson's Way; and in my studio/living room.

Use of color was methodically planned. All colors in each photo, from red sneaker laces to blue sky to yellow sweater, were coordinated and balanced. Two identical sets of clothes were selected for Brian to allow for stains and tears during the photo sessions. For the clock photos, a false-wall set was built and covered with wallpaper identical to that in Brian's room. This made it possible to control the lighting of each clock photo so that it would match the lighting in each accompanying photo throughout the day.

The photographs were taken using a Nikon FE2 with a 35, 50, 105, or 200mm lens. A blue color-correcting filter was used when appropriate. Available light was the primary light source. Reflectors were used to fill the shadows. For color temperature balance, multiple electronic-flash fill was used for natural tones and quartz-light fill for warmer tones. The film used was Kodachrome 64, processed by Kodak.

	DATE DUE	
	DISCARDED FROM THE	
	PORTVILLE FREE LIBRARY	
	6/10/24	

PORTVILLE FREE LIBRARY

PORTVILLE, N. Y.

Member Of
Chautauqua-Cattaraugus Library System